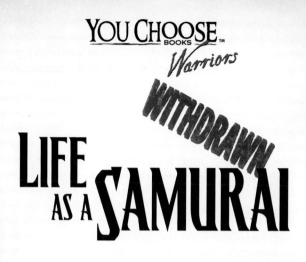

YOU CHOOSE BOOKS™

Warriors

WITHDRAWN

LIFE AS A SAMURAI

An Interactive History Adventure

by Matt Doeden

Consultant:
Don Roley
Ninjutsu Research Specialist
Colorado Springs, Colorado

CAPSTONE PRESS
a capstone imprint

You Choose Books are published by Capstone Press,
151 Good Counsel Drive, P.O. Box 669, Mankato, Minnesota 56002.
www.capstonepub.com

Books published by Capstone Press are manufactured with paper
containing at least 10 percent post-consumer waste.

Library of Congress Cataloging-in-Publication Data
Doeden, Matt.
  Life as a samurai : an interactive history adventure / by Matt Doeden.
    p. cm. — (You choose books: Warriors)
  Summary: "Describes the lives of samurai warriors in ancient Japan. The readers' choices
reveal the historical details of life as a samurai during the Gempei wars of the 1100s, the rise of
Nobunaga in 1560, and as a wandering ronin in the 1600s"—Provided by publisher.
  Includes bibliographical references and index.
  ISBN 978-1-4296-4783-0 (library binding)—ISBN 978-1-4296-5637-5 (paperback)
  1. Samurai—Juvenile literature. I. Title. II. Series.
  DS827.S3D64 2011
  952'.02—dc22   2010008884

Editorial Credits
Angie Kaelberer, editor; Bobbie Nuytten, designer; Wanda Winch, media researcher;
  Laura Manthe, production specialist

Image Credits
Alamy: JTB Photo Communications, 44, The Print Collector, 22; The Art Archive: Oriental
Art Museum, Genoa/Alfredo Dagli Orti, 33; The Bridgeman Art Library International:
©Look and Learn/Private Collection/ Dan Escott, 17, 37, Pat (Patrick) Nicolle, cover, 28,
Peter Newark Military Pictures, 12, Private Collection/H.M. Burton, 43; Courtesy of artist
Gary Hostallero, 78; Getty Images Inc.: Hulton Archive/Kusakabe Kimbei, 102; The Granger
Collection, 6, 55, 65, 94; Koninklijke Bibliotheek (Library of the Netherlands), Gedenkwaerdige
Gesantschappen (Memorable Missions, The Netherlands – Japan, 84; © Osprey Publishing,
www.ospreypublishing.com/Angus McBride, Samurai Heraldry/The Samurai, 40, 60; Peter
Newark's Pictures, 96; Shutterstock: Adam Hicks, 100, Mario babu, cover background, Radu
Razvan, 70; Stephen Turnbull Japan Archives, 82

Printed in the United States of America in Stevens Point, Wisconsin.
082011   006349R

TABLE OF CONTENTS

ABOUT YOUR ADVENTURE

YOU are living in Japan during a violent time in history. You are a samurai, one of Japan's great warriors. What battles will you fight? What decisions will you face?

In this book you'll explore how the choices people made meant the difference between life and death. Many of the events you'll experience happened to real people.

Chapter One sets the scene. Then you choose which path to read. Follow the directions at the bottom of each page. The choices you make will change your outcome. After you finish one path, go back and read the others for new perspectives and more adventures.

YOU CHOOSE the path
you take through history.

Samurai warriors were known for their skill, strength, and respect for honor.

JAPAN'S SAMURAI

Centuries ago Japan was a violent, unstable place. Powerful lords called daimyo fought long, bloody wars in their search for power and wealth. Secretive assassins called ninja prowled the night. Warrior monks combined battle with prayer. Foot soldiers called *ashigaru* fought with spears, bows, and other weapons. Exactly how this way of life developed isn't entirely clear. But the warriors who led the fighting are well known. They were the samurai.

Turn the page.

Warriors matching the description of samurai existed for centuries. But it wasn't until the 1100s that they were called samurai. The term "samurai" appeared as early as the 900s, but at first it referred to the emperor's servants. The word itself translates as "those who serve." In time the word became associated with those who served during times of war.

The role of the samurai changed over time. The earliest samurai were likely wealthy landowners who also trained in the art of war. Later the samurai became specialized warriors. By the late 1100s, the samurai rode on horseback and used bows and arrows as their main weapons.

Over the years war became a way of life in Japan. The period from 1467 until about 1600 is known as the Age of the Warring States. Powerful daimyo were at nearly constant war with one another. By this time the samurai sword had replaced the bow as the preferred weapon.

The samurai were officers and generals, leading huge armies into battle. Some were no longer content to remain tools of powerful daimyo. They seized power and became daimyo themselves, ruling their own lands and armies. Later many samurai who had either lost or left their masters struck out on their own. These wandering samurai were called *ronin*.

Turn the page.

The samurai were supposed to live by a strict code of conduct, although not all of them did. This code was called bushido, "the way of the warrior." It included such qualities as courage, respect, loyalty, and honesty. Above all else, the samurai valued honor.

Samurai warriors played a major role in almost every major conflict in Japan for more than 500 years. They helped shape Japan's history.

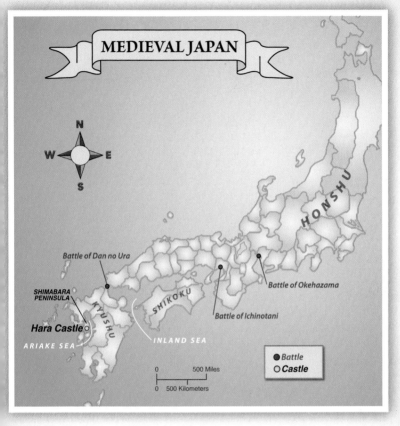

MEDIEVAL JAPAN

HONSHU

Battle of Dan no Ura

SHIMABARA
PENINSULA

KYUSHU

Hara Castle

ARIAKE SEA

SHIKOKU

INLAND SEA

Battle of Okehazama

Battle of Ichinotani

●	Battle
○	*Castle*

0 —— 500 Miles

0 —— 500 Kilometers

✤ To fight in the Gempei War in the late 1100s,
turn to page **13**.

✤ To stand with the daimyo Nobunaga during an
attack in 1560, turn to page **45**.

✤ To live the life of a wandering ronin in 1637,
turn to page **71**.

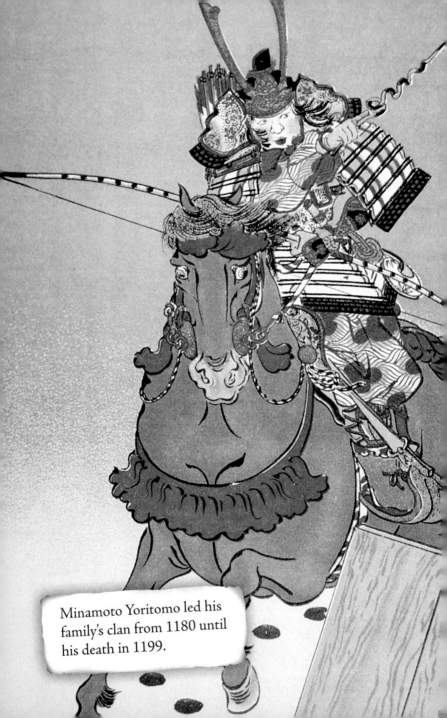

Minamoto Yoritomo led his family's clan from 1180 until his death in 1199.

CHAPTER 2

THE GEMPEI WAR

It is the spring of 1184. You ride through the night on your trusted horse. You come to the top of a steep hillside that overlooks a large fort called Ichinotani. Beyond the fort are the ocean and the ships of the Taira clan. The Taira have ruled Japan for nearly 30 years.

Minamoto Yoshitsune and his soldiers stand outside the fort. The Minamoto clan is a bitter rival to the Taira clan. Yoshitsune's brother Minamoto Yoritomo is the leader of the Minamoto clan. Yoritomo seeks to seize power from the Taira clan.

13

Turn the page.

High-ranking samurai from both sides have asked you to fight under their banners. Your family has ties to the Minamoto clan. Your father fought alongside Yoritomo's father during the Heiji Rebellion more than 20 years ago. The Taira destroyed the Minamoto forces in that battle. Your father was one of the few Minamoto samurai to survive.

Taira Kiyomori, the previous leader of the Taira clan, was a good and fair leader. Japan has rarely seen such good, stable leadership in recent times.

For more than 20 years, Kiyomori was the most powerful man in Japan. He was even more powerful than the emperor.

Before Kiyomori died in 1181, he turned over power to his son, Taira Munemori. You're not sure family ties are enough to make you fight against this ruling family.

→ To fight alongside the Minamoto clan, turn to page **16**.

→ To stand with the Taira clan, turn to page **18**.

Your family's honor is more important than anything else. You will not turn your back on a family friend in his time of greatest need.

As you ride toward the Minamoto camp, several samurai ride out to greet you. The camp buzzes with activity. The common soldiers are falling into ranks. Samurai on horseback are barking out orders.

Yoshitsune welcomes you. "We'll need all the help we can get," he says. "This is our chance to end this war. The Taira killed my father 25 years ago. I will finally get revenge for his death."

Yoshitsune explains the plan. Part of the army will attack the fort from the shore, drawing the enemy's attention. Then a small group of samurai on horseback will charge down the steep slope above the fort. They will attack from the rear.

Many samurai were
skilled at fighting
on horseback.

❧ To join the frontal attack along the shore,
turn to page **20**.

❧ To join the samurai charge from behind,
turn to page **22**.

You don't agree with the reasons for the Minamoto rebellion. Despite your family's connection to the Minamoto clan, you have to follow your heart.

You circle around the Minamoto camp and approach the fort. Guards outside look at you with suspicion.

"I've come to fight under the Taira banner," you tell them.

One of the guards leads you inside the fort to Munemori. He looks at you with tired eyes.

"I hope you're ready to fight," he says. "The Minamoto forces will attack soon. Ships are waiting nearby if we have to retreat."

Suddenly, a call rises up inside the fort. "The enemy is coming!"

You rush alongside Munemori to the front line. The sun has set. In the darkness, the battle is filled with confusion. Before you realize what's happening, the fort is on fire. "Samurai are attacking from the rear!" shouts a Taira soldier.

"Impossible!" someone barks back. "The enemy can't go over that steep cliff."

But it's true. The frontal attack was only a diversion. The Taira forces are completely unprepared for the attack from the rear.

"Retreat to the ships!" Munemori orders.

You've only been here a few hours, and you're already retreating. This is not what you had imagined.

➤ To follow orders and retreat to the ships,
turn to page **24**.

➤ To ignore the order and head into battle,
turn to page **25**.

Every samurai hopes to be the first into battle. Joining the force attacking from the front will allow you to do so. You report to Minamoto Noriyori, the samurai leading the charge. Your horse trots along at the head of the army.

As you come closer to the fort, you come upon a lone Taira samurai standing in your way. You could easily shoot him where he stands. Like all samurai, you're an excellent archer. But this samurai is not threatening you. He is armed, but he isn't even holding his weapon.

"Samurai!" the man cries, pointing at you. "I am Taira Mikoto. I have won many fights against men greater than you."

Mikoto is challenging you to single combat. Among samurai, victory in such a duel is one of the highest honors. But if you fight this man, you could die.

To accept the samurai's challenge of single combat, turn to page **27**.

To refuse, turn to page **32**.

Minamoto Yoshitsune led the attack on the Taira army.

"I would be honored to ride with you into battle," you tell Yoshitsune. He smiles and nods.

Several hours later, the sun has set, and you're back on your horse. You and a small group of mounted samurai wait atop the slope leading to the back of the fort. You keep out of sight. It's important that this attack be a complete surprise.

At last the main force begins its attack. You and the other horsemen carefully make your way down the slope. It is dark, and the footing is uncertain. But you make it down safely. No Taira forces lie in wait. They are all defending the fort against the attack from the front.

"Attack!" shouts Yoshitsune.

➤ *To set fire to the fort, turn to page* **30**.

➤ *To ride around to the main battle, turn to page* **35**.

The Minamoto have won this battle. You join the others heading for the ships. The Taira force quickly retreats to the island of Shikoku. The Minamoto forces have no chance to chase you. Even if they had the ships, they lack the sailing skill of the Taira clan.

After the battle Taira leaders try to use political power against the Minamoto. The 5-year-old emperor of Japan, Antoku, is the grandson of Taira Kiyomori. Antoku declares the Minamoto forces to be rebels and enemies of Japan. But that makes little difference. Minamoto's forces have the upper hand.

It's not too late to leave the war behind. Walking away now would be dishonorable. But you have a family you may never see again.

➺ To continue fighting, turn to page **39**.

➺ To abandon the Taira forces, turn to page **41**.

You came here to fight. You grab your weapons and charge toward the enemy line.

The situation is grim. Minamoto forces have used the confusion of the sneak attack to quickly advance on the fort. The disorganized Taira forces are falling back.

You draw back an arrow and let it fly into the enemy soldiers. You don't even bother to see whether you've hit your target. You shoot arrow after arrow, but the enemy keeps coming. Soon they're almost upon you. You draw your sword, called a *tachi*, and prepare to fight.

Turn the page.

An enemy samurai spots you and charges. The two of you circle one another. You make your move, but your enemy dodges the attack. He responds with a thrust that catches you across the shoulder. Blood runs down your arm as you try to catch your balance.

Just as your opponent is about to strike again, he stops suddenly and topples over. An arrow is lodged in his back. It's a lucky break for you. If there was anything you could have done here, that chance is now gone.

26

❖ To cut your losses and retreat, turn to page **31**.

❖ To continue fighting, turn to page **37**.

Nothing is more important to a samurai than honor. You get off your horse and set down your bow. Mikoto draws a long, curved sword called a tachi and stands before you. You draw your own sword. Your fellow samurai gather around. They understand the importance of single combat and will not interfere.

The two of you circle one another. You move forward, faking an attack, and then fall back. Mikoto lunges, but the tip of his sword comes up inches short of your armor.

For a split second, Mikoto is off balance. You thrust with your sword, aiming for a weak point in his armor. He barely manages to block the blow. You come at him again before he can catch his balance. Again he blocks your strike. He aims a low kick that knocks you to your knees.

Turn the page.

You scramble to get up, but Mikoto is upon you. Your swords clang loudly as you deflect his blows. He comes at you again with a desperate charge. You duck just in time as he swings for your neck.

Two samurai fought in single combat for the honor of their family and lord.

You bring the tip of your sword forward with a powerful thrust that pierces his armor. Mikoto falls to the ground, defeated.

You step back. The fight is over. You have won. Many samurai would take off his head, but you don't like that tradition. But you can't let Mikoto go free either. "You are my prisoner," you tell Mikoto as he hangs his head. You climb back on your horse, and the army continues its march.

➹ *Turn to page 43.*

The fort is the only advantage the Taira clan has. The best chance of victory is to burn it down. You get off your horse and gather kindling to start a small fire. Others are doing the same. Some men launch flaming arrows over the fence. Within minutes the crackling fire lights the sky.

You hurry back to your horse. The enemy is now in full retreat. As you ride, you come up alongside Yoshitsune. He looks at you and gives a short nod. Side by side, you charge into the battle ahead. Victory is at hand. It feels good to be on the winning side.

❧ Turn to page 43.

This isn't a fight. It's a massacre. Ignoring your orders was a mistake. The pain in your shoulder is the price you have paid for your decision. You turn and retreat before another of the enemy finishes the job and kills you.

The Taira ships return to the island of Shikoku. You'll stay there to recover. Your injury will heal in time. But you know that your arm will never be as strong as it was before. With your injury, no one would blame you for leaving the Taira army. But you can't bring yourself to do that.

31

➤ *Turn to page* **39**.

You see no reason to risk your own life by fighting Mikoto. "Get out of our way, or I'll shoot you where you stand," you shout.

Mikoto glares at you. "Coward!" he sneers.

How dare he call you a coward? You raise your bow and pull back an arrow. But Mikoto doesn't move. The arrow whistles through the air before slamming through Mikoto's leather armor with a thud. Mikoto never takes his eyes off you as he falls to his knees. Moments later, he is dead.

Minamoto Noriyori pulls alongside you on his horse. He looks at you with disgust. "Losing your temper that way shows you are without honor," he says. "Fall back. You don't deserve to be first into battle."

You do as you're ordered, knowing you'd be a fool to challenge him. You vow to prove yourself in the upcoming battle.

When the attack begins, the Taira are unprepared. Their army flees to their ships. Seeing several samurai racing toward safety, you charge. From your horse, you take aim and strike one of them with an arrow. You hit another and then another.

The Minamoto army attacked the Taira forces at Ichinotani.

Turn the page.

You scan the battlefield, searching for another target. Too late, you notice an enemy samurai taking aim at you. An arrow slams into your shoulder, knocking you from your horse. As you crash to the ground, another enemy is upon you. He raises a sword and brings it down upon your neck.

You die on the battlefield, knowing that your death is without honor. It is not the death any samurai would have chosen.

THE END

To follow another path, turn to page 11.
To read the conclusion, turn to page 103.

You live for the thrill of riding into battle. You urge your horse on as others set fire to the fort. The Taira forces are trapped between the flames and the Minamoto forces waiting outside.

As you round the corner of the fort, you prepare to charge. The flames light up a furious battle scene. Arrows fly from archers on both sides. You see several pairs of samurai in single combat, crossing swords in a battle for honor.

You draw your sword and ride into battle. You cut down one enemy after another.

Suddenly you feel a sharp pain in your right arm. An enemy arrow has hit you. Your sword slips from your grasp and falls with a clatter to the rocky ground.

Turn the page.

The wound is painful, but you'll survive. You clasp a hand over the wound to keep it from bleeding. You carefully guide your horse back behind the battle lines.

It is a major victory for the Minamoto allies. As the Taira ships sail away, you know it's only a matter of time before the rule of the Taira clan ends.

THE END

To follow another path, turn to page 11.
To read the conclusion, turn to page 103.

Warrior monks fought battles as well as serving as holy men.

Even with an injured arm, you know you're a better fighter than most of the enemy. With a shout, you race back into battle. A man charges at you. He wears a loose kimono and carries a *naginata*—a long pole with a sharp blade on the end. He is a warrior monk fighting for the Minamoto cause.

Turn the page.

The monk attacks. You swipe at his legs with your sword, but he easily dodges the blow. Your wound continues to bleed, draining your strength by the second.

Your opponent raises the naginata again. He buries the blade in your side. You crumple to the ground. In moments, you will be dead. But you take comfort in the fact that you fought to the end and never ran from battle.

THE END

To follow another path, turn to page 11.
To read the conclusion, turn to page 103.

You have pledged to fight for the Taira clan. You'd sooner die than break that oath.

Less than a year later, Taira and Minamoto forces meet again in the Battle of Dan no Ura. This time the fighting takes place at sea. You do your part by killing several enemy warriors. But the Taira forces are badly outnumbered. The Minamoto forces sweep through the Taira ships, cutting down warriors and soldiers. The battle turns the sea red with blood.

Around you, samurai are taking their lives rather than face defeat and dishonor. You watch with horror as the child emperor, Antoku, and his mother throw themselves into the sea. But you decide to keep fighting until the end.

Turn the page.

Just then an arrow strikes you in the chest. You fall into the red sea, grateful that you at least died honorably.

Samurai helped fight the Battle of Dan no Ura on the Inland Sea.

THE END

To follow another path, turn to page 11.
To read the conclusion, turn to page 103.

You won't give your life for a hopeless cause. You hope no one sees you leaving the camp, but you don't get your wish. Sasaki, a young samurai, spots you.

"Stop there," he calls. "Where are you going?"

"It's over," you tell him. "Come with me. You don't have to die here."

The young man looks at you with disgust. "What kind of samurai breaks his oath and runs from a fight?"

Sasaki draws his sword. "Die like a warrior," he says. But before he can come at you, your bow is ready. "Don't move," you say softly. "I don't want to shoot you, but I will."

Turn the page.

The young samurai hesitates. Then he charges, hoping to take you by surprise. He fails. You let an arrow fly. It catches him square in the chest. At such close range, his armor provides little protection. He clutches his chest and falls to his knees.

You leave Sasaki to die. As you walk away, you know your life will never be the same. Sasaki was right when he said that no samurai would behave as you have.

Your honor is gone, but you still have your life. Was it a good trade? Only time will tell.

THE END

To follow another path, turn to page 11.
To read the conclusion, turn to page 103.

The Minamoto attack is a huge success. As the fort burns, the Taira forces retreat.

The following year you fight at the Battle of Dan no Ura, which finishes off the Taira army. Seven years later, Yoritomo forces Emperor Go-Toba to grant him the title of shogun. This title gives him military control of Japan. Yoritomo rewards you for your loyal service. You serve him for the rest of your days.

Yoritomo became shogun in 1192.

THE END

To follow another path, turn to page 11.
To read the conclusion, turn to page 103.

Powerful daimyo Oda Nobunaga led an army against Yoshimoto.

CHAPTER 3

The Rise of Nobunaga

You sit on your horse and look over a low plain. Smoke rises from an enemy camp ahead of you. It is spring 1560, and you are in the middle of a war. You ride next to your daimyo, Oda Nobunaga. He is an intelligent, capable leader, but his army is small compared with the invading army you're watching.

Daimyo Imagawa Yoshimoto commands the invading force. Yoshimoto has mercilessly captured everything in his path and killed anyone who stood in his way. Now he seeks to take Nobunaga's lands.

45

Turn the page.

"The scouts say the enemy has 12 men for every one of ours," you say. "How can we hope to stand against such numbers?"

"We can't fight a frontal attack," Nobunaga answers. "We would quickly be overwhelmed. We can't surrender either. Yoshimoto is ruthless, and we would die as cowards."

"What then? We can't fight or surrender? What hope do we have?"

"We *can* fight," Nobunaga says. "We will not wait for the enemy to attack. They are overconfident. We must use that against them. We will bring the fight to Yoshimoto."

Nobunaga's plan is brilliant. You place your banners at a nearby temple. The bright banners will lead enemy scouts to believe that your main force is camped there. Then you will march under the cover of the forest to attack the enemy camp.

If you can take the enemy by surprise, you might just have a chance. It's a long shot, but it's the only shot you have.

Nobunaga expects you to play a major role in defending your homeland. You don't want to let him down.

❧ To lead a small scouting force, turn to page **48**.

❧ To lead the main attacking force, turn to page **50**.

As Nobunaga's main force gathers, you and another samurai, Suzuki, scout ahead on horseback. You're moving toward a small canyon near the village of Okehazama called Dengakuhazama. Yoshimoto's army is camped there. Water runs off your leather armor as you ride through a pouring rainstorm.

"This is a mission far better suited for ninja," says Suzuki. "They're made for sneaking around unseen."

"Nobunaga distrusts the ninja," you answer. "And so do I. Ninja use stealth and trickery. They don't have the honor of a samurai."

You move slowly as you approach the enemy camp. Through the trees, you see tens of thousands of men. They are celebrating, drinking rice wine called sake, and dancing.

"Now is the time for attack," Suzuki says.

You point to a large tent in the middle of the camp. "That is Yoshimoto's tent. An attack is only successful if we kill him. Without his leadership, his men will surrender quickly."

Suddenly you hear the snapping of a twig behind you. You bring your horse around in time to see an enemy running into the woods. He's seen you!

"We can't let him get back to his camp," you say.

"But we have to let Nobunaga know what we've seen here," Suzuki argues. "Any delay could be costly."

"We have to split up," you reply.

⇥ To chase the enemy through the woods,
turn to page **52**.

⇥ To return to Nobunaga to report what you've
discovered, turn to page **53**.

The greatest honor for any samurai is to be the first into battle. You can't pass up the opportunity to lead the attack.

The next day you march through the thick forest. Nobunaga's scouts report that Yoshimoto's forces are camped in a small canyon called Dengakuhazama near the village of Okehazama. The enemy leaders are celebrating their recent victories. They will be unprepared for battle. Even better, a steady rain will help cover your movements.

At last the enemy camp is within sight. You look behind you and see that your men are ready to fight. You adjust your helmet and grip your *katana* tightly.

"Attack!" you shout, and the army storms out from the trees. More than 1,000 of Nobunaga's best fighters rush into the enemy camp.

Your sneak attack has worked. Many of the enemy are unarmed. Some are drunk. Still others flee in the confusion.

Nobunaga's army is cutting through the enemy. But unless you can take down Yoshimoto and his officers, the attack will be meaningless.

➤ *To seek out minor officers on the field of battle, turn to page 54.*

➤ *To try to kill Yoshimoto, turn to page 56.*

"Go back and report to Nobunaga," you tell Suzuki. "I'll deal with this."

The enemy's tracks are clearly visible in the wet ground. You jump off your horse and chase the enemy on foot. You crash through trees and bushes. Branches slap your face. But you're in luck—you spot the enemy.

You dive at the man, knocking both of you to the muddy ground. He scrambles to his feet and draws a short sword. He is a common soldier and doesn't have your fighting skills. But you can't get to your sword from your position on the ground.

➸ To dive for the man's feet in hopes of throwing him off balance, turn to page **61**.

➸ To try to trick the man into letting you live, turn to page **63**.

52

"You make sure that soldier never reports us," you tell Suzuki. "I'll go back to camp."

When you reach the camp, Nobunaga and several of his top samurai are discussing plans for the attack. They look up as you approach.

"The time to attack is now," you tell them breathlessly. "Yoshimoto is busy celebrating."

Nobunaga strokes his long black mustache. "Then we march. Prepare the men!"

Nobunaga's small force organizes quickly. You all take cover in the woods. As you charge into the enemy camp, the enemy is stunned and is slow to respond. Nobunaga's forces hit hard. Enemy soldiers are dying or fleeing by the hundreds. Still, you know that killing enemy soldiers is pointless. You have to think bigger.

➤ *Turn to page* **56**.

You have to move quickly. If Yoshimoto's forces can organize, they will defeat you. A few enemy samurai are shouting commands. The soldiers around them are falling into rank. You can't let that happen.

You charge at one of the samurai. The man sees you coming, and you both draw your katanas. Everyone around recognizes two samurai engaged in single combat. No one moves to interfere.

With a cry, you strike at your opponent. He quickly steps aside. He uses your motion against you, tripping you and sending you sprawling to the ground. Your katana flies from your grasp and clatters to the ground several feet away.

The enemy sees that he has an advantage and springs on you. You have no sword. The only weapon you have is a double-edged knife called a *yoroi-doshi*.

Going up against a skilled swordsman with nothing but a knife seems risky. But you're not sure you could get to the sword in time.

Samurai used a variety of weapons in battle.

→ To draw the knife, turn to page **57**.

→ To try to grab your katana, turn to page **66**.

As long as Imagawa Yoshimoto is in command of his forces, you have no chance of real victory. Killing low-ranking samurai and soldiers will be meaningless.

Yoshimoto's tent is at the center of the camp. You and several other samurai head directly for it. A quick strike is important. If the enemy soldiers form ranks, you're doomed.

As you reach the tent, Yoshimoto himself steps outside. He yells at his men to stop fighting among themselves. You see the look of shock on his face as he realizes that he is the one under attack. You and your fellow samurai quickly surround the enemy leader.

➤ *To try to kill Yoshimoto, turn to page 59.*
➤ *To try to capture Yoshimoto, turn to page 67.*

There's no time to grab your katana. Instead you grab the yoroi-doshi, knowing that it will at least give you a chance.

The enemy samurai slashes at you as you scramble to your feet. But his sword thrusts wildly, and you dodge it easily. Again he attacks, thrusting his sword at your chest. You step to one side and throw out your leg in a sweeping kick. The kick catches him in the back of the leg, throwing him off balance. You leap at him, both of you crashing to the ground.

Turn the page.

Your enemy throws a powerful punch that lands under your chin and knocks the helmet from your head. You are dazed for a moment. He again thrusts his sword at your chest. As you dodge the blow, you move in closer. He flails, trying to put distance between you, but you thrust the knife into his throat. He falls to the ground, dead.

As you pick up your katana, a cheer goes up around you. "What happened?" you ask. One of Nobunaga's foot soldiers shouts the answer: "Yoshimoto is dead! Our samurai killed him outside his tent!"

With their leader dead, the enemy lay down their weapons and surrender. The battle is over. Despite being terribly outnumbered, Nobunaga has won.

➛ *Turn to page **69***.

Yoshimoto grips his sword as you and three other samurai close in. Two of the samurai break off to fight the enemy leader's guards. You and the other samurai deal with Yoshimoto.

The look in your enemy's eyes tells you that he knows he is beaten. Despite his huge advantage in numbers, Yoshimoto was unprepared. He will pay for his mistake with his life. Your friend and ally, Daisuke, moves in for the kill. He thrusts a spear at Yoshimoto's chest. But Yoshimoto's sword flashes as he deflects the blow.

With the impact, Yoshimoto spins toward you, momentarily defenseless. You waste no time. Your blade hums through the air as you swing, killing Yoshimoto instantly.

Turn the page.

Word quickly spreads that Yoshimoto and his generals are dead. Without a leader, many of the enemy soldiers surrender and vow to fight for Nobunaga instead.

Nobunaga's samurai killed Yoshimoto (right) in battle.

→ Turn to page **69**.

Your enemy does not have your warrior instincts. You have to take advantage while he is still unsure of himself.

In one swift motion, you roll and leap toward your enemy's feet. Any samurai would easily cut you down, but this man panics. He weakly thrusts the sword at you but misses. Your shoulder crashes into his knees as you wrap your arms around his legs. The man's sword flies from his grasp as he falls.

You briefly consider taking the man prisoner. But you don't have time to deal with a prisoner right now. Instead, you draw the dagger at your belt and ram it into the man's chest. It is the quickest death you can offer him. You hope he doesn't suffer long.

Turn the page.

You return to your own camp and join the army as it attacks Yoshimoto's camp. As you guessed, the enemy is totally unprepared. Imagawa Yoshimoto is killed in the attack, and his army falls apart. Most of them throw down their weapons and join forces with Nobunaga.

You know it's just the beginning for Oda Nobunaga. The daimyo is bound for great things, and you look forward to a life of serving at his side.

THE END

To follow another path, turn to page 11.
To read the conclusion, turn to page 103.

"Wait!" you shout. "You don't have to kill me. I'll let you go."

The man takes a step backward. You can tell that even though he has the upper hand, he has little interest in taking on a samurai in a fight.

The man turns and runs. He believed you! Of course, you are lying. You can't possibly allow him to return to camp. Lying wasn't an honorable thing to do. But what choice did you have?

You quickly pick up your sword and charge after your enemy. You catch him easily and strike. Your sword cuts into his right shoulder. The blow sends him sprawling to the ground, his sword flying out of his grasp.

Turn the page.

"You said I could go!" he screams. "I thought samurai were men of honor!"

"I am sorry," you tell him truthfully. This is not an action you're proud of taking. "I will end your pain now. Fighting me will just make it worse."

You take a step forward to finish the man. But as you raise your katana, he reaches into his belt and pulls out a small dagger. As the tip of your katana sinks into his chest, he flings the dagger at you. The weapon buries itself in your throat as you fall to the muddy ground.

You and your enemy die together in the woods. You managed to stop the enemy from spoiling the surprise attack, but you'll never know whether the attack was a success.

A samurai carried a
curved sword called a
katana close to his body.

65

THE END

To follow another path, turn to page 11.
To read the conclusion, turn to page 103.

Your fingers brush against the hilt of your katana, but you can't grasp the weapon before the enemy strikes. You try to roll out of the way of a sudden slash. The enemy's sword misses your neck. But it catches you on your left leg, leaving you bleeding heavily.

The enemy samurai approaches slowly. He knows now that time is on his side. With every heartbeat, more blood spills on the ground, and you grow weaker. The other samurai bows before finishing the job with a final stab of his sword. You feel almost no pain as you die on the Okehazama battlefield.

THE END

To follow another path, turn to page 11.
To read the conclusion, turn to page 103.

To follow another path, turn to page 11.
To read the conclusion, turn to page 103.

Nothing would humiliate Yoshimoto more than being captured. His army would fall apart. You motion to your fellow samurai to hold back.

"Surrender!" you shout to the enemy leader. "Give up and I will spare your life."

Yoshimoto glares at you with a sneer. "You are a fool," he hisses.

You approach him carefully. "Drop your weapon," you say.

With a flash, Yoshimoto and two of his guards are upon you. You barely have time to avoid a thrust aimed at your chest. Your friends charge in to help you, but it's too late. One of the guards pierces your chest with his spear, and you fall to the ground.

Turn the page.

As you lie there dying, you watch as your fellow samurai do the job you should have done in the first place. They kill Yoshimoto with one swing of a sword.

There is nothing anyone can do for you. You only hope that Yoshimoto's death will be enough to drive the enemy out of Nobunaga's lands. It's a shame you won't be around to see how it all ends.

THE END

To follow another path, turn to page 11.
To read the conclusion, turn to page 103.

Your role in the battle helped Nobunaga defend his lands and gain a powerful new army. Nobunaga wastes little time in using his newfound power. He marches the army to Kyoto. There he plans to unify all of Japan under his command.

Nobunaga quickly becomes one of the most feared and respected leaders Japan has ever known. You are one of his most trusted samurai. You have sworn an oath of loyalty to him. A samurai's word is his honor, and it is an oath you will never break. You know that you will continue to serve and protect him as long as he rules Japan.

69

THE END

To follow another path, turn to page 11.
To read the conclusion, turn to page 103.

Samurai sometimes fought with a long sword called a tachi.

CHAPTER 4

The Quest of the Ronin

You ride alone along a dusty road, your katana hanging from your belt. A small village lies ahead. The year is 1637, and you are in Japan's Shimabara Peninsula. Many people here have become Christians, even though a former shogun, Tokugawa Ieyasu, outlawed Christianity in 1614. The Tokugawa shogunate still seeks to remove the practice of Christianity from Japan. You are a faithful Buddhist, but you sympathize with the Christians who are being mistreated.

71

Turn the page.

You adjust your topknot. The hairstyle marks you as a samurai and serves as a warning to anyone who might think to challenge you. But while you are a samurai, you are without a master. You are a wandering swordsman—a ronin.

The Age of the Warring States is over. You and many others are without a place in Japan's new political system. Many of your fellow ronin have joined the Christian peasants in organizing a revolt. But you have little interest. You are on a warrior pilgrimage, known as a *musha shugyo*. Unlike the samurai of the past, your goal isn't to gain political power, land, or money. You fight for the pure honor and joy of fighting, hoping it will bring you enlightenment.

You ride into the village. Word has spread that ronin are gathering here to fight duels. Sure enough, you come upon a small gathering. Two ronin are fighting with the wooden swords now used in duels. You get off your horse and walk toward them. Another samurai greets you.

"My name is Saito," he says. "Have you come to fight?" You nod.

Just then, the duel ends. "Are you fighting today?" you ask Saito.

"No, I have other matters to attend to," he answers. "The local daimyo, Matsukura Katsuie, is heartless and cruel. I am part of a resistance movement against him. You should join us."

➤ To accept Saito's invitation, turn to page **74**.
➤ To focus instead on fighting duels, turn to page **76**.

"I have heard of Katsuie," you say. "I'm here to fight. It might as well be for a cause. I will join you."

Saito smiles. The two of you ride out of the village and head to nearby Hara Castle. There he introduces you to Amakusa Shiro, the leader of the revolt. You are surprised to discover that Shiro is only 16 years old. But even at such a young age, it is clear that he is a skilled leader.

"Another good sword is always welcome," he tells you. "We have attacked the enemy at several of his strongholds, but a huge Tokugawa force marches against us. All of our forces are falling back. We will make our stand here at Hara Castle."

Saito tells you that he's leaving Hara Castle to scout for enemy forces. "I could use your help on the mission," he continues.

❖ To join Saito on a scouting mission, turn to page **83**.

❖ To remain at Hara Castle and prepare for an enemy attack, turn to page **87**.

You politely turn down Saito's invitation. It is a worthy cause, but right now your only interest is in fighting.

Finding an opponent is easy. A young ronin agrees to your challenge. Villagers and other samurai gather around as the two of you face off with the wooden swords. You notice a much older samurai with a deeply scarred face in the crowd. He looks familiar, but you can't think of how you know him.

As the duel begins, the air snaps with the crack of the wooden swords against each other. Your opponent is powerful but too aggressive. You fend off or dodge one blow after another. Then the ronin comes straight at you with a thrust. He has pushed too hard and is off balance. You sweep your foot in a low kick that takes him down at his knees.

The onlookers roar in approval. Your gaze seeks out the old samurai you noticed before the battle. He is moving toward you. Suddenly you realize that you're looking at Miyamoto Musashi. He is the most famous of all ronin. He is now working for a clan, but he is still a legend.

"Well done," he says to you.

"Thank you, Musashi," you answer, filled with pride at the compliment.

"Will you fight me?" Musashi asks.

For a moment, you don't know how to respond. Miyamoto Musashi wants to fight you! It would be a great honor, but you also know that he is a skilled fighter who is capable of hurting you. Dueling samurai are supposed to pull away their swords at the last second, but Musashi doesn't always do this.

Turn the page.

Miyamoto Musashi was famous for fighting with two swords.

→ To accept the challenge, go to page **79**.

→ To decline, turn to page **81**.

You look Musashi in the eye. "I would be honored. I want to fight the best, and you are the best."

Musashi claps you on the shoulder as you step into the open space surrounded by the crowd. He draws a pair of wooden swords, one in each hand, and assumes a battle stance. Musashi is known for his fighting skill with two swords. You, like most samurai, use only one sword.

The fight begins slowly. The two of you circle one another, each faking attacks. Then Musashi comes at you. One of his swords hums through the air toward your head. Quickly you realize that this strike is a diversion. Musashi thrusts his other sword toward your chest.

Turn the page.

In one motion, you duck and bring your sword up in defense. One blow whisks over your head, while the other smashes into your sword. With both hands on your sword, you knock the sword from Musashi's hand.

Musashi appears to be taken by surprise. His guard is down. This is your chance! You could go for the easy strike to the neck. Or you could try to give Musashi a blow to the chest that would knock him down.

→ To go for the easy strike, turn to page **89**.

→ To try to knock Musashi to the ground, turn to page **90**.

You are no match for Musashi. Fighting him with no hope of winning seems foolish.

"I must say no," you answer. "I've fought already today. Once is enough."

You ride away from the village, alone once again. Later that day you arrive in yet another small village. You come on a scene that shocks you. Tokugawa forces are in the town collecting taxes. They have captured two Christians. Even though the religion is common in this part of Japan, the shogun has declared it a crime.

You watch in horror as the two men are strung up on crosses and crucified. Their deaths make you realize just why the rebellion Saito mentioned is brewing.

Turn the page.

It's not too late to join the rebellion. Soldiers are gathering under a young leader named Amakusa Shiro at nearby Hara Castle. You could still use your skills to fight for a cause.

Christian rebels carried flags with crosses as they battled for Hara Castle.

❖ To ride to Hara Castle and fight, turn to page 87.

❖ To continue on your journey, turn to page 92.

"I'm with you," you tell your new friend.

The two of you take off on horseback. You ride south along the coastline of the Ariake Sea, which the enemy forces will have to cross by ship. Soon you see signs of an enemy camp. Several ships are out at sea. Some of them appear to be European. The Dutch have been trading heavily in this area. Is it possible that they are helping the Tokugawa forces?

Saito also sees the ships. "Why would the Europeans help the shogun?" he wonders out loud. "Aren't they Christians? Shouldn't they be on our side?"

You shrug. "I'm not sure. The Europeans will do anything for a trade agreement. I guess money is more important to them than their god."

Turn the page.

Dutch traders used their ships to help Tokugawa forces during the rebellion.

You ride inland a bit to stay hidden, but you know that you're risking being captured. "Should we turn around?" you ask.

"We need to know what we're up against," Saito answers. "We have to keep going."

But you're not the only scouts in the area. Without warning, an arrow whizzes past your head. An enemy scout has spotted you.

"Fall back," Saito shouts. But before he can move, another arrow catches him in the chest. He slumps and falls to the ground, blood trickling from his mouth.

Your friend is dead. If you stay here, you might be next.

➤ *To retreat to Hara Castle, turn to page **86***.

➤ *To attack the enemy scouts, turn to page **93***.

There's nothing you can do here. Saito is dead, and the Tokugawa forces are closing in fast. You turn your horse around and race back toward Hara Castle. You haven't learned much about the size of the Tokugawa force, but maybe the information about the Dutch ships will be useful.

You return safely to the castle and report what you saw. Shiro's generals shake their heads at the news that the shogun might be allied with the Dutch. It means that the enemy will have cannons and plenty of gunpowder. It's bad news for the rebellion.

You join others in building up the castle defenses. Part of your job is to take apart ships and use the wood to strengthen the castle walls, which are in poor repair. Everyone works hard, knowing that this likely will be the rebellion's last stand. If the Tokugawa troops take Hara Castle, it will be over, and nothing will have changed.

In January 1638, the siege begins. Cannons fire at the castle day and night. You have fewer weapons than the enemy troops. There is little you can do to fight back.

Turn the page.

Soon the cannon fire stops. This is when the real siege begins. The Tokugawa forces are well supplied, but your soldiers are cut off from any supply lines. Food and what little gunpowder you had stocked are quickly running out. The enemy doesn't need to keep attacking. They just have to wait for your supplies to run out.

A small group of rebels is planning a raid on the enemy camp. You can go with them if you wish.

→ To take part in the raid, turn to page **97**.
→ To stay with the castle defenders, turn to page **99**.

You won't see another opportunity against a fighter as great as Musashi. You lunge forward, striking a blow to Musashi's sword.

Your eyes lock with Musashi's. But it is not honor, respect, or even fear you see in the other man's eyes. It's disgust. Musashi has tricked you into thinking he was defenseless. Your opponent spins in a flash, avoiding your attack. Before you can regain your balance, he lands a crashing blow to your head. You fall to the ground as the world slowly turns black.

Musashi kneels beside you. "I'm sorry," he whispers. "But you knew the risk in fighting me." They are the last words you will ever hear.

THE END

To follow another path, turn to page 11.
To read the conclusion, turn to page 103.

You pounce on Musashi, slashing at his chest in order to knock him to the ground. But too late you realize that Musashi has tricked you. He's not off balance at all. His trick has caused you to lose your mental focus. A good samurai should never lose focus.

Musashi steps aside, and your wild attack comes up empty. Now you're the one off balance. You try to spin away from him, but the flat end of his sword smashes against your right wrist. The impact of the blow forces you to drop your sword.

Just like that, the duel is over. In past centuries a defeated samurai would have been honor-bound to take his own life rather than live in defeat. But times have changed. You are honored just for having fought one of the greatest swordsmen in Japanese history.

Later that day you ride away from the small village. You lost a duel today, but the fighting was good and honorable. But you also know that you have much further to go before you find enlightenment.

THE END

To follow another path, turn to page 11.
To read the conclusion, turn to page 103.

As you ride down a narrow dirt road, you realize how tired you are of fighting. You had a chance to duel one of Japan's greatest samurai and said no. And now you realize that battle, even for a noble cause, no longer appeals to you. Perhaps the life of a samurai is not for you. After all, you have no master, and you seem no closer to enlightenment.

There are many options for a ronin who has grown tired of fighting. You could take up farming. You could join a Buddhist monastery and spend your days seeking enlightenment as a monk. Whatever you decide, your fighting days are over.

THE END

To follow another path, turn to page 11.
To read the conclusion, turn to page 103.

"No!" you shout with rage. Another arrow whistles past your head as you spring into action. Instead of turning and riding away, you spur your horse in a gallop toward the scouts. A charge would be the last thing they would expect.

You quickly close ground on a single enemy scout. The man is frantically trying to ready his bow for another shot, but you're too fast. Your katana hums through the air, striking the man's arm. It slices deeply into his flesh, and the bow drops to the ground. The man screams in pain before you finish him with a killing blow.

Turn the page.

The noise has attracted attention. You hear voices shouting in the distance. The sound of hooves tells you that more enemies on horseback are nearby. It's too late to run, and you have no hope of holding back all of your enemies.

Samurai used bows and arrows to attack enemies from a distance.

You stand your ground and vow to fight to the end. But the enemy does not have a fair fight in mind. Archers take aim at you. An arrow pierces your arm, and then another catches you in the leg. You fall to your knees, still grasping your katana. The sword never leaves your grasp as an arrow to the chest finishes you.

You have failed in your mission. You hope Shiro and the rebels fare better.

THE END

To follow another path, turn to page 11.
To read the conclusion, turn to page 103.

Tokugawa Ieyasu died in 1616, two years after he outlawed Christianity in Japan.

Life inside the castle during the winter has been harsh. Food supplies are low. The rebel soldiers are becoming discouraged. You jump at the chance to join a raiding party. You hope to find some supplies and take out some Tokugawa forces along the way.

You and a small force of rebels move on foot under the cover of night. You stay silent as you prepare to strike.

At last you attack. The small rebel force sweeps into an enemy camp. The element of surprise works in your favor. Guns fire and swords clash as you quickly overrun the camp.

97

The enemy is slow to respond, and you begin to retreat to the castle. But since you were on the front lines of the strike, you are one of the last to retreat.

Turn the page.

Before you can return to the safety of the castle, an enemy gunshot catches you in the back. You fall to the ground, struggling to breathe.

You know that your wound is deadly. As you lie there dying, you listen to the sounds of battle around you. You don't know whether your fellow rebels can win the war, but at least you'll die knowing that you won this battle. That is good enough for you.

THE END

To follow another path, turn to page 11.
To read the conclusion, turn to page 103.

The rebels carry out several successful raids, killing large numbers of enemy troops and even taking some supplies. But in the long term, the raids are little more than a nuisance to the Tokugawa forces. Their numbers are more than 100,000—almost four times the rebel force.

The winter months make life difficult for both sides. But spring finally brings an end to the siege. On April 12, 1638, the enemy troops begin their final assault. The castle falls three days later. You fight to the end, swinging your katana in a hopeless attempt to fight back the enemy. But it's a battle you cannot win.

Turn the page.

Ronin were without masters. They traveled the country alone.

As you slash at an enemy warrior, a bullet catches you square in the chest. You fall to the ground, dead. Later the enemy forces burn Hara Castle to the ground. You and thousands of your fellow rebels are buried beneath the ruins of the castle.

THE END

To follow another path, turn to page 11.
To read the conclusion, turn to page 103.

The samurai continued to fight for Japan until the late 1800s.

CHAPTER 5

THE SAMURAI'S PLACE IN HISTORY

People are still fascinated by the way the samurai lived their lives. The samurai blended a warlike nature with a sense of honor, tradition, and family. The samurai could be ruthless killers. But at the same time, they were bound by honor and the code of bushido. Under the code, a samurai's oath was sacred. Many preferred to take their own lives rather than live with the shame of defeat.

The samurai's rise to power began in the late 1100s after the Gempei War. At that time Minamoto Yoritomo made himself Japan's first shogun. Any daimyo who wanted to hold or expand his power then needed the samurai. The samurai helped shape the politics and culture of the nation for the next 700 years. Most samurai loyally served their masters. Their oath of loyalty was a bond they would not break.

The rise of Oda Nobunaga marked the beginning of the decline of samurai power. After defeating Imagawa Yoshimoto in 1560, Nobunaga changed the face of Japanese politics. He and his successor, Toyotomi Hideyoshi, started to unify the empire. Under their powerful rule, the Age of the Warring States came to an end. Japan was unified around 1600.

As the fighting ended, the role of the samurai changed quickly. Daimyo no longer needed the samurai. Masterless samurai roamed the countryside as ronin, battling one another just for the honor of doing battle. Some still served the empire. Others traveled to other countries to fight. Still others left war behind and became farmers, writers, or monks.

Samurai numbers continued to decline over the next 150 years. By the 1860s Japanese soldiers were training in Western fighting methods. In 1873 Emperor Meiji abolished the class of samurai in Japanese society. The age of the samurai was over.

But the image of the samurai as the noble and skilled warrior lives on. The memory of their honor, discipline, fearlessness, and might still stands as a symbol of pride to the Japanese people.

Timeline

1100s—The term *samurai* is first used to refer to a highly trained soldier.

1180—The Gempei War begins.

1184—Minamoto Yoshitsune defeats the Taira clan at the Battle of Ichinotani.

1185—The Gempei War ends after the Minamoto clan defeats the Taira clan at the Battle of Dan no Ura.

1192—Minamoto Yoritomo becomes the first shogun of the Kamakura shogunate.

1274—The Mongol Empire launches an attack on Japan. Samurai and daimyo band together to repel the attack.

1281—The Mongol Empire stages another attack on Japan. After three months of fighting, Japan's samurai drive them away once again.

1467—The Onin War begins, starting the Age of the Warring States. Samurai become an important resource to any daimyo wishing to take new lands or hold his own.

1534—Oda Nobunaga is born.

1549—Shimazu Takahisa becomes the first samurai to use European guns in battle during the Siege of Kajiki.

1560—Oda Nobunaga defeats the much larger force of Imagawa Yoshimoto at the Battle of Okehazama. With the victory, Nobunaga begins his quest to unify Japan.

1584—Miyamoto Musashi, the most famous of the ronin, is born.

1600—As Japan is unified, the Age of the Warring States ends. Many samurai find themselves without masters and choose to live as ronin.

1637–1638—Thousands of ronin join with Christian peasants of the Shimabara Peninsula in a revolt against the rule of the Tokugawa Shogunate and the local daimyo. The revolt is finally put down in the bloody siege at Hara Castle.

1700s—The role of the samurai in Japanese culture gradually decreases.

1873—Emperor Meiji abolishes the samurai as a separate class of Japanese society.

OTHER PATHS TO EXPLORE

In this book, you've explored the life of the samurai at several important events in Japanese history. You've seen that samurai were fierce warriors and great generals. You've learned about their dedication to honor.

Perspectives on history are as varied as the people who lived it. You can explore other paths on your own to learn more about what happened. Seeing history from many points of view is an important part of understanding it.

Here are some ideas of other points of view to explore:

+ Samurai went through intense training in fighting styles, weapons, and combat tactics. What would it have been like to train to be a samurai?

+ Some samurai left Japan to fight abroad. What might life have been like for a samurai who traveled to China or Europe to fight?

+ At times the ranks of the samurai were open only to the wealthy. What options might a warrior of lower class have had?

READ MORE

Dean, Arlan. *Samurai: Warlords of Japan*. New York: Children's Press, 2005.

Guillain, Charlotte. *Samurai*. Chicago: Raintree, 2010.

Leavitt, Caroline. *Samurai*. Mankato, Minn.: Capstone Press, 2007.

Park, Louise, and Timothy Love. *The Japanese Samurai*. New York: Marshall Cavendish Benchmark, 2010.

INTERNET SITES

FactHound offers a safe, fun way to find Internet sites related to this book. All of the sites on FactHound have been researched by our staff.

Here's all you do:

Visit *www.facthound.com*

Type in this code: 9781429647830

GLOSSARY

ashigaru (ah-shee-GAH-roo)—a peasant soldier in Japan

bushido (buh-SHEE-doh)—the samurai code of honor

clan (KLAN)—a large group of related families

daimyo (DIME-yoh)—a powerful landowner in medieval Japanese society; daimyo were similar to lords in medieval Europe

enlightenment (en-LITE-uhn-muhnt)—the realization of a truth, especially a spiritual truth

katana (kuh-TAHN-uh)—a commonly used type of long sword in medieval Japan; a katana has a slightly curved blade

ninja (NIHN-juh)—a warrior who relied on stealth and secrecy to perform missions, such as spying, assassination, and battle

110

ronin (ROW-nin)—a samurai who is without a master

shogun (SHOH-guhn)—a military commander in medieval Japan

siege (SEEJ)—an attack designed to surround a place and cut it off from supplies or help

tachi (TAH-chee)—a sword often carried by samurai; a tachi was curved like a katana, but was longer

BIBLIOGRAPHY

Deal, William E. *Handbook to Life in Medieval and Early Modern Japan.* New York: Oxford University Press, 2007.

Jansen, Marius B., ed. *Warrior Rule in Japan.* New York: Cambridge University Press, 1995.

Louis, Thomas, and Tommy Ito. *Samurai: The Code of the Warrior.* New York: Sterling, 2008.

Time-Life Books editors. *What Life Was Like among Samurai and Shoguns: Japan, AD 1000–1700.* Alexandria, Va.: Time-Life Books, 1999.

Turnbull, Stephen R. *Warriors of Medieval Japan.* New York: Osprey Pub., 2005.

Turnbull, Stephen R. *Samurai: The Story of Japan's Great Warriors.* New York: PRC Publishing, 2004.

INDEX